GREAT EXPLORATIONS

EDMUND HILLARY

First to the Top

Dan Elish

 Marshall Cavendish
Benchmark
New York

Marshall Cavendish Benchmark
99 White Plains Road
Tarrytown, NY 10591-9001
www.marshallcavendish.us

All Internet sites were available and accurate when the book was sent to press.

Library of Congress Cataloging-in-Publication Data

Elish, Dan.
Edmund Hillary : first to the top / by Dan Elish.
p. cm. — (Great explorations)
Summary: "An examination of the life and accomplishments of the famed
explorer from New Zealand who was one of the first to scale Mount
Everest"—Provided by publisher.
Includes bibliographical references and index.
ISBN-13: 978-0-7614-2224-2
ISBN-10: 0-7614-2224-2
1. Hillary, Edmund, Sir—Juvenile literature. 2. Mountaineers—New
Zealand—Biography—Juvenile literature. I. Title. II. Series.

GV199.92.H54E55 2007
796.52'2092—dc22

2005027929

Photo research by Anne Burns Images

Cover photo: Corbis:Charlie Munsey
Cover inset: Corbis/Hulton Deutsch Collection

The photographs in this book are used by permission and through the courtesy of: *Corbis:* Wild Country, 5, 42;
Macduff Everton, 11; Hulton Deutsch Collection, 13; Bettman, 21, 36, 61. *Rex Features:* 6. *Getty Images:* 8, 32, 40,
44, 55; Hulton Archive, 59. *AP Wide World Photos:* 10, 29, 34, 64, 67, 69. *Library of Congress:* 15. *The Image
Works:* Topham, 17, 39, 50; Science Museum/Topham, 24; Mary Evans Picture Library, 27; SSPL, 46. *Royal
Geographic Society:* 19, 25, 52, 62. *Woodfin Camp:* Scott Fischer, 47; Neal Beidleman, 57.

Printed in China
1 3 5 6 4 2

Contents

foreword

One hundred million years ago an ocean separated what is now India from the rest of the Asian continent. Over the next 60 million years, India slowly inched its way across the open water and eventually rammed into the mainland. This formed a giant mountain range called the Himalayas. Spanning 1,500 miles (2,415 kilometers), the Himalayas are home to many of the world's highest peaks. At 29,035 feet (8,856 meters) above sea level, Mount Everest is the tallest of them all.

Spread between the nations of Tibet and Nepal, Everest remained largely unknown to the Western world for many years. It was not until 1921 that mountaineers first tried to climb it. Many failed and turned back. Others died on its icy peaks. To conquer the mountain, climbers had to negotiate severe cold, possible avalanches, and moving glaciers of solid ice. They also had to climb with the knowledge that the higher they reached, there would be less and less air to breathe.

Mount Everest. The great mountain stands so tall that there is a dropoff of a mile (1.6 kilometers) on either side of the summit.

Despite the obstacles and often overwhelming odds, brave mountaineers kept on trying. It was not until 1953 that a beekeeper from New Zealand named Edmund Hillary and Sherpa Tenzing Norgay, a climber from a village at the base of the mountain, finally reached the top. It was an incredible achievement. Today, experienced guides and modern equipment are available to help climbers more safely and easily make their way up an established route in their quest for the summit. But Hillary, Norgay, and the members of their British expedition had to blaze their own course up the mountainside, stretching the limits of known human endurance.

foreword

Edmund Hillary in a recent photograph. He once said, "I have modest abilities. I combine these with a good deal of determination, and I rather like to succeed."

When Hillary and Norgay reached the peak, they became instant celebrities. But Edmund Hillary never allowed his newfound fame to cloud his perspective on the feat. "I was just an enthusiastic mountaineer of modest abilities who was willing to work quite hard," he has said. "It was the media that transformed me into a heroic figure."

To his credit, Hillary has used his fame to raise money for schools and hospitals for the Sherpa people who live at the base of mountain. As more and more people have attempted Everest, Hillary has also led movements to make sure the mountain remains clean and unpolluted. Most important, Edmund Hillary has personified a special kind of heroism—a humble man who achieved his goals through a combination of hard work, a deep love of climbing, and joyous enthusiasm.

As climber Don George has said, "Here is a someone who did the near impossible, climbing the world's tallest mountain, and then did the near impossible again—refusing to be spoiled by all the adulation and accolades that achievement earned him, and remaining loyal to an ideal and a people he loved." This spirit and daring have earned Edmund Hillary a place among the ranks of the world's greatest explorers and adventurers.

ONE

A Boy Who Loved Books

Long before Edmund Hillary discovered his love of mountain climbing, his passion was books. The story goes that young Edmund loved reading so much that he convinced his older sister June to warn him when his father was going to make one of his frequent late-night bed checks. First, Edmund ran a long string down the hall from his room to June's. He then crawled into bed and looped the string around his toe. When June would hear their father headed down the hall, she would pull the string. By the time his father reached his room, Edmund had time to flip off the light, close his book, and pretend to be asleep.

Due in part to this fondness for literature, Hillary grew up with an extremely active imagination. Later in life, he recalled the youthful flights of fancy that were spurred by his love of reading:

There was a phase when I was the fastest gun in the west, then

Growing up, Edmund Hillary was a shy boy who loved books. He said, "I certainly never was a happy teenager."

another when I explored the Antarctic. I would walk for hours with my mind drifting to all these things. . . . My mind would be miles away and I would be slashing villains with swords and capturing beautiful maidens and doing all sorts of heroic things.

But despite his dreams of heroism, Edmund did not seem destined for great adventure. Born on July 20, 1919, Hillary spent the bulk of his childhood in the rural town of Tuakau in New Zealand, a small country off the eastern coast of Australia. His mother, Gertrude, was a schoolteacher. His father, Percival, founded a weekly newspaper, the

Tuakau District News, and served as its chief reporter, typesetter, and managing editor all rolled into one. The newspaper was printed on a press in a shed on the Hillarys' small farm.

Though Edmund played sports with his younger brother Rex, Edmund was short, slight, and uncoordinated for his age. He was so skinny that a gym teacher once cast a single look in his direction and fumed, "What will they send me next!"

Faced with such criticism, the boy often withdrew. As Hillary put it years later, "I was a shy boy with a deep sense of inferiority that I still have."

Still, there were signs of the great determination that helped drive him to the top of the world's highest mountains. Hillary's father was a tough disciplinarian—as Edmund put it, "a very firm man." Though his father loved to build things with the children and was an expert story-teller, he would not shy away from taking one of his children to the woodshed for a spanking if he felt it was deserved. Hillary later recalled:

> *I always felt my father wanted me to admit that I'd done wrong, and one thing I'm rather proud of, whether it's good or not, is that . . . I never agreed that what I'd done was wrong—whether it was wrong or not. I think this stubborn[n]ess carried me through my other adventures in life.*

Hillary's sister confirmed her brother's view, saying, "Much of Edmund's determination came from standing up to his father."

Still, Hillary admired both of his parents enormously, calling them "people of very strong character." The 1930s were the years of the Great Depression, and Hillary's father was outraged by the horrible state of the working poor. His mother would often ask her three children to clean their plates, saying, "Remember the starving millions in Asia." As

A group of Sherpas enjoys some time away from the mountain.

an adult, Hillary did remember. Perhaps his most lasting legacy is not conquering Everest but the work he has done for the Sherpa people in the Himalayas.

In part because Hillary's mother was a teacher, Edmund excelled in school. With his mother's coaching he became the best student in the Tuakau primary school eventually skipping a few grades. At age eleven, Edmund passed the admission test to a prestigious grammar school in Auckland. He was soon taking the train to the city—two hours each way—reading a book a day to pass the time. His first few years at the new school were rough. Not only was Edmund the youngest student there, but the school had much tougher academic standards than the one in Tuakau. He was often forced to miss the last train to make up work in French, his weakest subject. Socially, he was a disaster. As Edmund said, "I had no friends whatsoever."

But slowly things began to change for the bookish loner. First, he grew. Five inches one year. Four the next. As Hillary became stronger and taller, his confidence soared. Then when Hillary was sixteen, his life took another dramatic turn for the better. He discovered his real true love: the great outdoors.

It happened on a class trip to Mount Ruapehu, south of Auckland. Hillary's gangly frame had grown muscular. Though Edmund was not a natural athlete in terms of the types of sports that require good eye/hand

At 9,200 feet (2.8 kilometers), Mount Ruapehu is the tallest mountain on the North Island of New Zealand.

Arctic Explorers

Edmund Hillary was born just after the great age of arctic exploration. In 1909, after years of trying, Robert E. Peary reached the North Pole. Then in 1911, Roald Amundsen of Norway and four companions became the first people to travel to the South Pole.

Four years later in 1915, Ernest Shackleton led a crew of twenty-eight men on an expedition to the South Pole. But his ship, the *Endurance*, was crushed by the arctic ice in the Weddell Sea. Showing remarkable leadership, Shackleton was able to guide his men to an icy refuge on a desolate strip of arctic land called Elephant Island. From there, Shackleton and five of his crew set out on a life boat across the cold, stormy sea in search of a distant whaling station 700 miles (1,127 kilometers) away. The voyage took seventeen days. The boat was nearly capsized by large waves. Miraculously, Shackleton and crew made it safely. A couple of months later, Shackleton rescued the rest of his crew from Elephant Island. All twenty-eight men survived.

Ernest Shackleton, whose ship the Endurance is shown
here, was one of Hillary's heroes. "Whenever he was in a
difficult circumstance," Hillary said, "he seemed to have
the great ability to inspire his men and lead his party
safely out of those conditions."

coordination, as he took to the mountain paths, he was pleased to discover that he had much greater stamina than his classmates.

This was the first time I had even seen snow, because we didn't get it in Auckland, and for ten days I skied and scrambled around the hills. It was the most wonderful experience I'd ever had up to that stage, and I think it really was the beginning of my enthusiasm for mountains and for snow and ice. In fact, it was really the first real adventure I'd had.

At home, Edmund told his parents, brother, and sister all about his time at Mount Ruapehu, exaggerating many of the details. Fueled by his new love of the outdoors, Hillary found new heroes to look up to—men such as Ernest Shackleton, the great explorer of Antarctica who had led twenty-eight men safely back to civilization after his ship, the *Endurance,* was crushed by polar ice. "Whenever he was in a difficult circumstance," Hillary has said of Shackleton, "which he frequently was, he seemed to have the great ability to inspire his men and lead his party safely out of those conditions."

These are leadership qualities that Hillary himself would develop later in life. But in high school, his charisma was still not readily apparent. Because his growth spurt had made him one of the larger boys, he was appointed sergeant of the number one platoon in his school's army battalion. But when drilling his troops in their formations, Hillary would become nervous and issue the wrong commands. Luckily, his soldiers learned to ignore him and march in the correct direction no matter what he said. Later, Hillary put it this way:

There are some people who are natural leaders, who have the ability to think quickly or choose the right decisions at the right moment. But I think there are an awful lot of us who have to learn how to be a leader, and in actual fact, I believe that most people, if they really want to, can become competent leaders.

By the time Hillary was sixteen, he had grown tall, lean, and strong. He found he had great endurance when it came to climbing mountains.

Through experiences at school, Hillary was beginning to turn himself into a "competent" leader. But it would take a while longer before he had the chance to put those skills to the test. When Hillary graduated Auckland Grammar School, he did not set out to climb the Swiss Alps or to explore the Arctic. At the insistence of his parents, he enrolled in a university.

T W O
The Young Mountaineer

Hillary's primary education was followed by an uncertain future. As he wrote in his book *High Adventure,* "It took two years of university life to convince my parents that I was unsuited to an academic career."

Despite being a bright and curious young man, the future explorer was just too restless at that time in his life to give his full attention to detailed lectures on subjects such as solid geometry. A few years earlier, Hillary's father had left his job with the *Tuakau District News* and became a full-time beekeeper. Yearning to spend more time outdoors, Edmund decided to go into the family business. It was hard, unpredictable work. As Hillary put it, "a constant fight against the vagaries [whims] of the weather and a mad rush when all our 1,600 hives decided to swarm at once." Even so, the job and lifestyle were exactly what Edmund was looking for. In his free time, he would tramp through the hills that surrounded his family farm.

Hillary in a typical climbing outfit of the day,
including an open-circuit oxygen tank.

In 1939 New Zealand was drawn into World War II, and Edmund briefly considered joining the air force. Though he finally decided to stick with beekeeping, Hillary was becoming restless. After a period of particularly hard work, Edmund convinced his father to grant him a well-earned vacation. One of Edmund's stops was a famous tourist resort called the Hermitage in the heart of New Zealand's Southern Alps. As Hillary and his travel companion, a friend named Brian, drove into the heart of the great mountains, Hillary grew more and more excited. Upon arriving, he set out immediately on a hike toward the first snow he could see. The peak turned out to be much farther than he had thought. But even though he was stumbling over loose rocks in light shoes, he kept on going until he reached the top.

That evening in the lobby of the Hermitage, Edmund was still reeling from the thrill of the climb. Suddenly, two men entered. The room grew silent. Lingering nearby, Hillary heard one of the men say, "I was pretty tired when we got to the icecap, but Harry was like a tiger and almost dragged me to the top." Years later, Hillary found out that the two men were Harry Stevenson and Doug Dick, two of the most well-known climbers in all of New Zealand. At the time, Hillary was slumped in the corner feeling thoroughly jealous, excluded from all the fun that the two climbers seemed to be having. It was then that Hillary made a simple but life-changing decision: he would take up mountaineering.

The next day, Hillary and his friend set out to climb Mount Olivier. At first, their guide, an older man with a decidedly round belly, set too slow a pace up the mountain. Impatient, Hillary dashed ahead on his own, moving quickly through the cool, crisp air, enjoying a wonderful sense of freedom. After a fast lunch (of boiled goat) and a swim in a cold mountain lake, they resumed their hike, climbing rapidly up a tall snowy slope. Near the top, once again Hillary could not stick to the guide's pace and scrambled as fast as he could toward the peak. It was

One of Everest's early pioneers, Frank Smythe was the author
of twenty-seven popular books about climbing.

the first of many summits he would reach. "And next day I returned home," Hillary wrote, "but my new enthusiasm for the mountains went home with me and gave me little rest in the years that followed."

As Hillary became more and more obsessed with mountaineering, he found new heroes to look up to. One was Frank Smythe, who had made it 28,000 feet (8,540 meters) up the north side of Everest. Another was Eric Shipton, a British climber who was one of the first men to explore the Himalayas.

He also found a new career. In 1942, at age twenty-three, Hillary joined the military and became a navigator in the New Zealand Air Force. The rugged military life suited him well. While in the Fiji and the Solomon islands in the Pacific Ocean, Hillary took time to hike, fish, and explore. He even became an expert crocodile hunter, once killing an 8-foot (2.4-meter) specimen. When the war ended in 1945, Hillary continued to look for new adventures. One of his plans was nearly fatal. When he and a friend rode a repaired motorboat through rough waters, one of the gas tanks broke loose, sending a fire roaring through the engine. Preparing to jump off the boat, Edmund was flung backward into the flames before plunging into the salt water. In agony, the two men somehow managed to swim the 500 yards (458 meters) to shore, where two American sailors rushed them to a naval hospital.

Once Hillary had recovered from his injuries, he focused on improving his mountaineering skills. Although he had climbed many small peaks and a few big ones, he still knew little about the technical side of the sport. In 1947 Hillary became good friends with Harry Ayres, New Zealand's best-known mountain climber. Over the next three years, Ayres instructed Hillary in the subtleties of ice and snow climbing. Then in 1950, a climbing friend named George Lowe rekindled a dream Hillary had been secretly harboring for years. One day, as the two men were climbing down a New Zealand glacier, Lowe suddenly said, "Have you ever thought about going to the Himalayas, Ed?" In

Hillary studies the Tasman Glacier with fellow climber Harry Ayres.

fact, Hillary had—many times. As early as 1940, Hillary had told a friend, "Someday I'm going to climb Everest." Of course, at the time, no one had believed him. But underneath Hillary's modest, unassuming façade, was a deeply driven, determined person.

Though it took some time to raise the necessary funds, Hillary, Lowe, and a team of New Zealand climbers first made their way to the Himalayas in 1951. After a train ride through India, they spent weeks investigating high peaks that no one had climbed before. Deep into their journey, they heard some exciting news: a trip was being planned for the autumn of 1951 to explore a new approach to Everest. As an added bonus, the expedition was to be lead by Eric Shipton himself—one of Hillary's heroes. Though Edmund was desperate to be invited to join the trip, he did not think he had a chance to be asked. But word of his mountaineering skill had spread. Later, Hillary described what happened next:

> *We returned to Ranikhet [in India] thin and wasted and without a penny in our pockets. . . . As we entered our hotel, unshaven and dirty, we were handed a cablegram. It was an invitation to two of us to join Eric Shipton's party.*

Edmund Hillary was being given a chance to realize his dream. He was going to Everest.

THREE

"Because It's There"

By the time Edmund Hillary was invited to join Eric Shipton's expedition to Everest, climbers had been trying to reach the peak for many years. The quest first began in 1820 when a group of British surveyors set out to map and measure the Himalayas. But since neither Nepal nor Tibet allowed Westerners within their borders, the surveyors were forced to take their measurements from more than 100 miles (161 kilometers) away. As a result, it was not until 1852 that what had been named Peak XV (or Peak 15) was measured as standing a stunning 29,002 feet (8,846 meters) high—the highest point on Earth. (Everest's current height is thought to be 33 feet [10 meters] higher, at 29,035 feet [8,856 meters]). Though the people of Tibet called the mountain Chomolungma, or "goddess mother of the world" and the Nepalis called it Sagarmatha, "goddess of the sky," the British ultimately named Peak XV after Sir George Everest, the surveyor general of India from 1830 to 1843.

Sir George Everest was a military engineer who was appointed to be the surveyor-general of India in 1830. In 1852 he became the first man to successfully measure the famous mountain that would bear his name.

Once Everest was measured and named, the biggest problem facing potential climbers was simply gaining access to the mountain. When Robert Peary claimed to have reached the North Pole in 1909 and Roald Amundsen led an expedition to the South Pole in 1911, interest in reaching the top of Everest—known as the third pole—grew. It was not until 1920 that top-level diplomats were able to sway the spiritual leader of Buddhism, the Dalai Lama. He eventually granted a British party permission to visit Tibet to see if a route up the mountain was possible. Since Tibet lay on the northern side of the mountain, Everest's first explorers were forced to find their way to the top from the north.

In May 1921 a small expedition gathered in Darjeeling, India, under the leadership of Colonel C. K. Howard-Bury, an Irish aristocrat. But as the trip went on, George Mallory, a schoolmaster from England, ended up assuming the lion's share of responsibility for the trip. Though the explorers barely even made it onto the base of the mountain before being driven back by a blizzard, Mallory saw what they had come to find: a possible route to the top.

Encouraged, Mallory returned to the mountain the following year. Though horribly underdressed in tweeds, Mallory and two other men reached an elevation of 26,985 feet (8,225 meters). After a night of heavy storms, Mallory decided to make a final push for the summit, which lay only 2,000 feet (610 meters) beyond. But tragedy struck. The

George Mallory and fellow climber Edward Norton set a new world altitude record on the north face of Mount Everest in 1922.

Up and Down

When asked why he wanted to climb Mount Everest, George Mallory uttered these famous words: "Because it's there."

Still, debate has raged over whether Mallory and his climbing companion, Sandy Irvine, reached the summit of the great mountain before they disappeared. Most climbers agree that they did not. But one person who is not particularly concerned one way or the other is Edmund Hillary.

If he had succeeded in getting to the top I think it would be fantastic. However, I have always felt that you haven't completed the job on the mountain until you get safely to the bottom again, so even if they had discovered that Mallory had been first to the top, I could at least claim I had been the first person to get to the top and then safely down.

Hillary makes a valid point. Many climbers have reached Everest's summit, then died on the way down.

climbers set off a massive avalanche that swept seven Sherpa porters to their deaths. The intrepid climbers decided to turn back. Wracked with guilt, Mallory refused the chance to lead another expedition two years later. But the lure of the great mountain was too strong, and he eventually decided to make one more attempt at the summit. On June 8, 1924, Mallory and an Oxford student named Andrew "Sandy" Irvine made a push from 28,128 feet (8,579 meters) for the peak. Last spotted at one o'clock that afternoon "going strong for the top," they were lost on the icy mountain. Though Irvine's body has never been found, Mallory's was discovered in 1999.

Over the next twenty-six years, many other expeditions attempted to scale the north side of Everest. In 1934 an Englishman named Maurice Wilson decided to crash a plane at the base of the mountain and climb up from there. Though he was not allowed to fly into Nepal, Wilson

Two aviators gaze down at Everest's peak from a Westland biplane in this illustration from 1933.

eventually landed in India, snuck into Tibet and made it to 27,000 feet (8,235 meters) before freezing to death. Most other expeditions took more conventional approaches. Still, none got closer than 1,000 feet (305 meters) from the summit. Then in 1950, the political climate in Nepal changed, and the country opened its borders to foreigners. After years of failing to climb the northern side of the mountain, Eric Shipton was given the honor of leading the first expedition to look for a route from the south.

Edmund Hillary and Earle Riddiford, the other New Zealander lucky enough to be picked to join the expedition, arrived in Lucknow, India, on August 28, 1951. After a long trip by train, canoe, and foot, they finally met up with Eric Shipton and the rest of the climbing party near the Indian-Nepalese border two weeks later. Then came a long trek to the base of Everest during periods of pouring rain. Shipton, Hillary, and the rest of the expedition tramped along muddy tracks, crossed surging rivers, slipped down hills, and were plagued by leeches. Through so many trials, Hillary soon discovered that nothing fazed Eric Shipton. "Sitting in his sleeping bag, with his umbrella over his head to divert the drips," Hillary wrote of a night spent in heavy rain, "he puffed at his pipe and read a novel in the flickering light of a candle. He could not have looked more contented in an easy chair at home in front of a cozy fire."

Pushing on, the expedition reached mountain country in late September. They made their base camp at the foot of the Khumbu Glacier and got ready to hack out a route to the top. At that point, the only picture the group had of the southern part of the mountain made the slopes look impossibly steep. It was an image so daunting that the men called it "the horror photograph."

Hillary and crew were right to be intimidated. Due to the presence of two mountains, Lhotse and Nuptse, that lie on Everest's southern flank, the only path to the base of Everest itself was through the Khumbu Icefall. This extremely treacherous stretch of terrain is marked

Between treacherous crevasses and huge blocks of ice called seracs, most climbers find the Khumbu Icefall to be the most technically challenging part of the route up Everest. The glacier there moves 3 to 4 feet (0.9 to 1.2 meters) a day.

by giant crevasses, or chasms, and even larger seracs—tall, unstable blocks of ice. Writer and climber Jon Krakauer, described the fearful icefall like this:

> *Because the climbing route wove under, around, and between hundreds of these unstable towers, each trip through the Icefall was a little like playing a round of Russian roulette: sooner or later any given serac was going to fall over without warning, and you could only hope you weren't beneath it when it toppled.*

It did not take long for Hillary to get a powerful reminder of just how dangerous the Khumbu Icefall could be. On his first trip up, an entire sheet of ice broke into large blocks and started sliding straight toward a giant crevasse. Attached by rope to three other team members, Hillary hit the ground and planted his ax in the ice. This quick thinking stopped Hillary and his teammates from being dragged into the crevasse. All four men survived—but not before one teammate, Riddiford, dangled over the edge of the chasm.

In the end, Hillary and his teammates were able to struggle up the icefall and plot a possible route to the summit. Later, Eric Shipton worried about the risk of having Sherpa porters carry supplies across the difficult Khumbu Icefall. Hillary realized that "the only way to attempt [Everest] was to modify the old standards of safety and justifiable risk and to meet the dangers as they came; to drive through regardless."

It was that attitude that would help him reach the top. But Hillary's chance would have to wait. Winter was fast approaching. Having shown that it was possible to navigate the first stretch of the mountain, Shipton decided to turn back and wait to make another attempt in the spring of 1953. But on the way home, the team received some bad news: the Nepalese government had granted a group of Swiss climbers permission to make an attempt at the summit in the spring of 1952.

A Climbing Culture

The Sherpas are a small sect of devout Buddhists whose ancestors migrated to the base of the Himalayas about five centuries ago. Because the rocky terrain of the Himalayas does not lend itself to farming, Sherpas historically herded yaks and traded between Tibet and India. Today, the Sherpa culture is directly tied to the mountain they still call Chomolungma. Raised at altitudes of 9,000 (2,743 meters) to 14,000 feet (4,267 meters), Sherpas adapt well to the high elevations of Everest. In modern Sherpa culture, the best climbers are the most esteemed people in a village. A young man hoping to make a career on the mountains will try to join an expedition as a kitchen boy or porter and then, over time, hope to be promoted to climber or guide.

It is a dangerous profession. Between the years 1920 and 1996, fifty-three Sherpas died on the mountain. But most Sherpas feel that the rewards are worth the risk. As Premnuru, a Sherpa cook, said, "More expeditions means more jobs for Sherpas."

Eric Shipton was the only veteran of all four attempts to reach Everest's summit in the 1930s. Here he leads the 1951 expedition up the Khumbu Icefall.

But once again, the final 1,000 feet (305 meters) of Everest would prove to be too much. In May 1952, two members of the Swiss team reached 28,210 feet (8,604 meters) but then were forced to turn back.

Chomolungma remained unconquered, and Hillary and crew would be offered another chance to be the first to reach the top.

FOUR
"Expedition/ Phase One"

As the team of climbers prepared for their 1953 expedition, the British organizing committee realized that the only way to conquer a mountain as formidable as Everest was to send a large, well-provisioned expedition with a strong leader at the helm. Though Eric Shipton's mountaineering expertise was unquestioned, the committee came to feel that he did not have the all-consuming drive necessary to get to the summit. They turned instead to a military man named Colonel John Hunt.

When Hillary heard the news, he was furious. How could an Everest expedition not include Eric Shipton, the greatest Himalayan explorer of his time? But the newly appointed Hunt quickly proved his competence. "Evidence of Hunt's caliber was not long in appearing," Hillary wrote, "for the post [mail] brought a series of detailed plans which I reluctantly had to admit seemed to hit the nail on the head every time."

Hillary (right) with expedition leader John Hunt. Hunt wrote that the 1953 expedition was inspired by the "persistence" and "determination" of "earlier Everest climbers."

When the group gathered in Kathmandu in early March, Hillary was immediately impressed by Hunt's energy, commitment, and his promise to "lead the expedition from the front." It was at the same meeting that Hillary first met the man who would accompany him to the top: Sherpa Tenzing Norgay.

Like many male Sherpas of his generation, Tenzing had pursued a career in the mountains from a young age. In 1933 Norgay migrated from his home village in Nepal to Darjeeling, India, in the hope of getting hired to be a porter for that year's British Everest expedition. Two years later, at age twenty-one, Norgay was picked by Eric Shipton to join a team set to explore the Everest region. Over the course of seven expeditions, Norgay fell under the great mountain's powerful spell. "I could not say no," he said about accepting a job on an early and risky expedition. "For in my heart I needed to go, and the pull of Everest was stronger for me than any force on earth." In 1952 Norgay was with Raymond Lambert, of the Swiss team, when freezing cold forced them to turn back a mere 825 feet (252 meters) from the summit. Though Norgay felt great loyalty to Lambert, he could not resist giving the mountain one last attempt with the British. At their first meeting, Hillary immediately picked up on Norgay's "quiet air of confidence." Hillary was also pleased with the choices for the other members of the expedition, a cross section of the most experienced Himalayan climbers in the world, including his good friend from back home, George Lowe. But no matter how high the level of talent that had been assembled, Hillary was well aware of the difficulties ahead. Later he wrote:

> *The Swiss parties had been strong ones, well equipped and well organized—and yet they had failed. It is not necessary to find excuses for not climbing Everest—the mountain will supply those in abundance. But if we were to have any chance of success, our expedition would need a high degree of well-acclimatized technical skill; it would need the best modern equipment and oxygen; and it would need first-class organization. But more than anything else, it would need its share of good luck.*

Hillary's view was shared by the rest of his team. They approached the mountain with guarded confidence but also with great respect. Reaching the summit, they realized, would not be an easy task.

Today, most Everest expeditions start their journey with a short

Hillary (left) was pleased to have old friend George Lowe (right) on the expedition. When Lowe saw Hillary coming back down the mountain after his historic climb, Lowe rushed to meet his friend with mugs of hot soup.

plane ride from Kathmandu to the Lukla airport which lies on the foot of the Himalayas at 9,000 feet (2,745 meters). In 1953, however, the airport did not exist. Hillary and the rest of the expedition had to begin their journey with a 170-mile (274-kilometer) trek just to reach the Everest region. Once settled in Base Camp at the Thyangboche Monastery, the climbers spent from March 30 until April 6 hiking up to elevations reaching 20,000 feet (6,100 meters) in order to allow their

THIN AIR

Adjusting to the thin air, or acclimatization, might well be the most difficult thing climbers have to accomplish if they hope to make it to the top of a mountain as high as Everest. At 17,000 feet (5,185 meters), the altitude of the Thyangboche Monastery and Hillary's Base Camp, there is approximately half the amount of oxygen in the air than there is at sea level. On the mountain's summit, there is only a third as much. If someone was simply dropped by a plane onto Everest's peak with no chance to acclimatize, he or she would pass out and die within five or ten minutes. Even at 17,000 feet (5,185 meters), a full 12,000 (3,660 meters) feet beneath the summit, climbers routinely feel nauseated or short of breath, and suffer horrible headaches.

Luckily, the human body can adjust to higher altitudes. Over time, a climber's blood begins to carry more oxygen-bearing red blood cells. But there are still considerable risks. A climber on a mountain such as Everest is always in danger of suffering High Altitude Cerebral Edema or HACE, a condition that occurs when fluid leaking from blood vessels causes the brain to swell. When this occurs, if a victim is not evacuated to a lower altitude, he or she will most likely die. Climbing Everest is dangerous business, indeed.

bodies to slowly adjust to the change in altitude. Team member Tom Bourdillon instructed Hillary and the others in how to use the oxygen tanks they would need above 26,000 feet (7,930 meters). Because Hillary had spent the better part of the past two years in the Himalayas, the altitude at Base Camp was not a problem for him. One of the reasons Hillary was such a skilled climber might have been his natural ability to function in thin air. Years later, Hillary said, "You're so much slower in higher altitudes . . . but I used to keep moving pretty steadily most of the time and I didn't stop too often for panting and puffing . . . I was very fit in those days."

Hillary's ability to climb well in thin air did not go unnoticed by John Hunt. After acclimatizing, Hunt asked Hillary to find a way through the treacherous Khumbu Icefall to the Western Cwm, a broad glacial valley that was the next section of the mountain to be climbed on the way to the summit. Though Hillary was thrilled to get the assignment, he was dismayed to discover that the icefall was in even worse condition than it had been back in 1951. It had been split by "innumerable crevasses and menaced by crumbling ice towers," the climber noted. Undeterred, Hillary and his team started out; and several difficult and perilous days later, they had forged a workable, if dangerous, route up to the Western Cwm. This was just the first step in a larger plan. The expedition's strategy was to pitch a series of camps up the mountain and to use Sherpa porters to keep them provisioned. With any luck, they would be able to set up a final camp within striking distance of the summit.

Now that the team had established a route through the icefall, it was time to take on the Western Cwm itself—a section of the mountain that could become unbearably hot as the sun reflected off the icy slopes. During one work period, Hillary described it as "an absolute inferno."

It was during this leg of the journey that Hillary had the chance to work with Tenzing Norgay. Paired up, the two men took turns blazing the trail up the mountain. Then a near tragedy brought the men even closer. Along the Khumbu Icefall, Hillary leaped across a wide crevasse and landed forcibly on the other side. With a sudden crack, the side of the crevasse snapped off and he slid into the chasm. In a flash, Hillary jammed his cramponed boots into one side and braced his shoulder against the other. Up above, Norgay also acted quickly. He embedded his ice ax in the snow and looped the rope that was attached to Hillary around it. Tenzing's quick thinking broke Hillary's fall and possibly saved his life. Later, Hillary wrote that Norgay's "rope work was first class, as my near-catastrophe had shown. . . . Best of all, as far as I was

Camp Five in the Western Cwm, high in the clouds.

Hillary and climbing partner Tenzing Norgay. Norgay said of the top of Everest, "It was such a sight as I had never seen before and would never see again: wild, wonderful and terrible."

concerned, he was prepared to go fast and hard."

In Norgay, Hillary had found a friend and a kindred climbing spirit. Again, John Hunt must have noticed. On May 7, the expedition leader gathered the group and announced who would be the lucky climbers to get a chance at the summit. The first opportunity was given to Charles Evans and Tom Bourdillon, two strong English climbers. If they did not succeed, the second attempt would go to Hillary and Norgay.

FIVE
The First Team Fails

Though Edmund Hillary was an excellent climber, he never would have been able to reach the top of Everest by himself. One of the earmarks of the 1953 British expedition was its extraordinary teamwork. In a later interview, Hillary praised the group:

> *Without a doubt our greatest strength on Everest in 1953 was our very strong team spirit. Individually, as mountaineers, we were not particularly expert people. We were competent climbers, but we worked together, and we were determined that someone should get to the top. All of us, of course, wanted to be that one, but it was even more important that someone in the group reach the summit.*

Each man wanted to be the first to climb to the summit. But no one let his personal desire to reach the top overshadow the ultimate goal of the mission.

The treacherous Lhotse face. As writer Jon Krakauer put it,
"I quickly came to understand that climbing Everest was
primarily about enduring pain."

Once the party had established a series of camps to the top of the Western Cwm, the next section of the mountain to be conquered was the Lhotse Face, a wall of glacial ice that rises 3,700 feet (1,129 meters) at 40° to 80° inclines. The steepest sections are nearly vertical. Today, the entire route is secured with fixed ropes. In 1953, of course, this expanse of ice was completely bare.

Faced with such a challenge, the team that had been assigned to forge a path up this difficult section of the mountain soon became worn out. In the cold, thin air, a climber named Michael Westmacott was unable to drive himself above the height of 23,000 feet (7,015 meters). Another named George Band caught a bad cold. At this point, George Lowe, Hillary's climbing buddy from New Zealand, and a Sherpa named Ang Nyima, took it upon themselves to push the mission forward.

By May 11, Lowe and Nyima had completed the backbreaking task of cutting steps in the ice and laying fixed ropes part way up the Lhotse Face, transforming a highly difficult route into one that could be more easily climbed. After establishing Camp 6 at 23,000 feet (7,015 meters), Lowe was joined by Wilfred Noyce. The two men pushed to the top of the Lhotse Face and set up Camp 7. On May 15, Hillary, Noyce, and three Sherpas hauled provisions up to this new camp. Hillary was thrilled to note that he was moving well at 24,000 feet (7,320 meters) without oxygen. "I could, if necessary," he wrote, "have gone on a great deal farther." Though 5,000 feet (1,525 meters) away, the summit felt all too close.

The climbers would have to wait. Colonel Hunt's strategy called for the two summit teams—Evans and Bourdillon, then Hillary and Norgay—to conserve their energy at the lower altitudes of what came to be known as Advance Base Camp located on the Western Cwm at 21,200 feet (6,462 meters). While Hillary and Norgay rested, others forged a path from the top of the Lhotse Face to a section of the mountain called the South Col. From May 16 through 19, Hillary and the

Sherpa Tenzing Norgay spoke seven languages but never learned to write. He dictated several books about his famous ascent of Everest.

other members of the two summit teams watched and waited from below as the workers on the upper reaches of the mountain tried unsuccessfully to carve out a route. Four days passed with no progress because the climbers were hampered by high winds. Clearly, the effort up top was undermanned. Though Hillary begged permission to go up and help, Hunt refused, determined to keep the summit teams rested.

To add to the team's worries, time was running out. The expedition had to get near the summit soon. Due to the harsh weather conditions, Everest can be climbed only during a few weeks of the spring and parts of the late summer. After delays, Hunt had no choice but to initiate the next phase of the operation—carrying supplies up to the South Col— even though the climbers above had not yet been able to forge a path there. On May 20, Wilfred Noyce led nine Sherpa porters up to Camp 7. The next day, when Hillary offered to help the push up the mountain,

Hunt agreed. On May 22, Hillary, Norgay, and a team of Sherpas cut a path up to the base of the South Col. Later, on the way down the mountain to rest, Hillary and Norgay passed Evans, Bourdillon, and Hunt on their way to make the first attempt at the summit.

Hillary and Norgay did not have long to rest back at the lower altitudes of Advance Base Camp. In case Evans and Bourdillon failed, Hillary and Norgay had to be waiting at one of the upper camps within range of the summit. Using oxygen to maintain their strength, Hillary and Norgay climbed back up to Camp 7 the next day. There they spent the night with a group of Sherpas and George Lowe and Alfred Gregory, who had been sent along to provide support. The next morning, the team ascended to 25,000 feet (7,625 meters). Hillary was admiring the view and nibbling on a piece of chocolate when he heard Lowe shout and saw him pointing. High above, walking along a ridge that joined the South Col to the south summit, were Evans and Bourdillon. Hillary was thrilled. They were close to the top. But Norgay was strangely silent. Hillary did not realize then that Norgay felt that a Sherpa should be one of the first men to step on Everest's summit.

In addition to Evans and Bourdillon's fine progress, Hillary and Norgay pushed even farther up the mountain. The next major obstacle was the dangerous Geneva Spur, a 2,000-foot (610-meter) steep slope of snow-covered black rock. Again, today the spur is equipped with fixed ropes. But Hillary and his crew dragged themselves up without the aid of ropes, using whatever hand- and toeholds they could find in the rock. At the top of the spur, they looked up at what remained of their challenge. Later, Hillary wrote, "Towering above our heads was our mountain, looking depressingly steep and formidable."

That awesome task was the next day's challenge. Hillary and Norgay soon came upon Camp 8, their resting spot for the night. Moments after they arrived, Colonel Hunt and Sherpa Da Namgyal came stumbling back to the camp from farther up the mountain. Realizing that

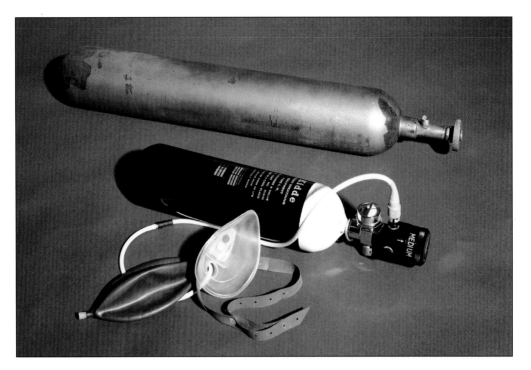

Better equipment helped Hillary and Norgay reach the summit. Here an oxygen cylinder from 1922 (top) lies next to the more modern tank and breathing mask used by the members of the 1953 expedition.

Hunt's condition was desperate, Hillary ran up to meet them with a fresh bottle of oxygen. Later, while Hunt was recovering in one of the small tents, Lowe shouted, "They're up! They're up!" Indeed, Evans and Bourdillon were visible again, this time moving up the south summit at an elevation of 28,700 feet (8,754 meters)—higher than anyone had ever been before. Still, Hillary knew that Evans and Bourdillon had to be low on oxygen. It was also late in the day. With daylight running out, they might not have time to reach the summit and make it back down before nightfall. Even though both men were, as Hillary put it, "sensible chaps with a keen desire to go on living," he knew that both men's desire to reach the top might cloud their ability to make good decisions. Today, the final 3,000 feet (915 meters) of Everest is referred to as the

The south summit in 1996. The next day, a fierce storm claimed
the lives of many of the climbers in this picture.

Death Zone—a place where the air is so thin and temperatures are so frigid that it is nearly impossible to think clearly.

Back at camp, Hillary and the others could do nothing but sit and wait. After fixing the tents to make sure that they were secure for the night, the ever-observant George Lowe caught sight of Evans and Bourdillon descending. Moments later, the two brave climbers limped back to camp, literally covered with ice. Though exhausted, they had found two tanks of oxygen that the Swiss expedition had left in the snow the year before. Evans and Bourdillon left them where they had found them on the mountain for Hillary and Norgay to use the next day. Back in the tents with cups of hot tea, the two men told their story. On top of the south summit, with the peak of Everest in view, they had to decide whether to go on or turn back. The fresher of the two, Bourdillon, wanted to go on—alone, if necessary. But Evans eventually convinced him that to continue would be madness. They did not have the strength, oxygen, or daylight to make it to the top and back down again. Bourdillon had reluctantly agreed.

After a chilly night, Hunt decided that he would accompany Evans and Bourdillon farther down the mountain. Before he left, Hunt told Hillary of his moral duty to reach the top of the mountain—for the sake of the British empire and all of the brave mountaineers who had come before him. Then Hunt handed Hillary a small white crucifix and asked him to leave it on the summit.

Hillary and Norgay set off up the mountain to establish their final camp. Since many of the Sherpas were feeling the strain of the high altitude and were unable to climb higher, both Hillary and Norgay had to haul up to 50 pounds (22.7 kilograms) of supplies. When they came to a pile of extra oxygen tanks and a spare tent that Colonel Hunt had left behind, they carried them along, too. Again, George Lowe had done a fine job, forging a path up the side of the mountain.

Soon the mountaineers were so exhausted that Hillary wrote, "each

THE SHERPA SPIRIT

The evening before his famous summit attempt, Hillary witnessed a shining example of the remarkable work ethic and loyalty of the Sherpa people. After helping Hillary and Norgay get settled at their final camp, Sherpa Ang Nyima asked Hillary if he could spend the night there—even though he was running dangerously low on oxygen—in order to help them prepare for their final push for the top in the morning. Later Hillary remembered,

> *This demonstration of loyalty and unselfishness from a man who was obviously going to have great difficulty in getting down at all affected me deeply and seemed to epitomize all that is best in the Sherpas.*

Nyima was willing to risk his own life for the good of the mission. But Hillary refused his generous offer, and Ang Nyima got back down the mountain safely.

step became a separate entity—a major task that was going to require a maximum of effort." Completely worn out, the climbers began to look for a small section of ice that was flat enough to serve as the final camp from which Hillary and Norgay would make their push to the summit.

Hillary and Norgay faced many challenges on their final push to the summit.

But every spot that looked promising from a distance turned out to be far too angled or uneven for a tent to stand on. Desperate, Norgay remembered a place 50 feet (15.2 meters) above and to the left that he and Raymond Lambert had noticed a year earlier on the Swiss expedition. Norgay led Hillary and their team through waist-deep snow only to find that the area he had in mind was too small. It was then that George Lowe noticed a spot overhead. Pushing up the mountain, they came to a small ice shelf—slanted but usable. As Hillary and Norgay got to work with their axes, cutting away ice to make the ledge more level, Lowe and the others hurried back down the mountain so they could reach the lower camp before nightfall. After struggling nearly until dark to secure their small tent on the icy slope, Hillary and Norgay crawled inside it and began the long wait until morning.

SIX

Going for the Top

Inside their small tent, Hillary and Norgay shared a meal of chicken noodle soup, sardines, biscuits, dates, canned apricots, and pints of a hot lemon drink doused with sugar. Once they were nourished, the two men turned to a bigger problem. At that high an altitude, the only way to sleep without freezing, possibly to death, is to breathe oxygen. Hillary and Norgay had only four hours' worth of oxygen to spare for the night. So the two men connected their oxygen masks to one partially used tank and dozed from 9:00 until 11:00 p.m. When the tank was empty, they woke up shivering. To fight the cold, they drank hot lemonade until 1:00 in the morning. Then they hooked up the second oxygen tank and dozed again until 3:00 a.m. At 4:00, they forced themselves out of their sleeping bags into the cold dawn and started to get ready.

Before he had retired for the night, Hillary had faced a dilemma. Should he wear his boots inside his sleeping bag or should he sleep in his socks? Later Hillary wrote, "the flesh is weak and I decided on a comfortable night." So he took off his boots. In the morning, Hillary discovered that he had made the wrong choice: his boots had frozen solid during the night. Hillary's only recourse was to place a small stove between his knees and thaw his boots in its heat. Ignoring the smell of melting rubber, Hillary finally got his boots warm enough to slip on his feet. After putting on every article of clothing that they had with them and checking each other's oxygen sets, Hillary and Norgay looked to the summit and set off.

Since Hillary's boots were still stiff, Tenzing Norgay took the lead up a very steep slope. On either side were drop-offs of more than 1,000

Two climbers cross a log bridge over a crevasse in the Western Cwm. On their ascent to the summit, Hillary and Norgay knew this part of the mountain was stretching ominously below.

feet (305 meters) to the Western Cwm. At 28,000 feet (8,540 meters) they looked up to see the south summit directly overhead. They were making good time. But as Hillary took the lead, the two climbers ran into a mountaineer's curse—snow with a breakable crust. Every few steps up the steep slope, Hillary's leg broke through the snow's outer crust, and he sank to his knees. It was a tiring and awkward way to climb. But they had no choice. After struggling up the mountain for an hour, Hillary and Norgay finally mounted a small crest. In a small hollow below them was a welcome sight: the two Swiss oxygen tanks left by Evans and Bourdillon, both almost completely covered with snow. The dials revealed that both tanks were one-third full and could be used later on to aid Hillary and Norgay's descent—a lucky break.

There was still plenty of toil ahead, and more hard work beyond that. Next, Hillary and Norgay faced a steep snow-covered slope some 400 feet (122 meters) high. Taking the lead, Norgay sank to his ankles on his first step. On the next, to his knees. Then to his waist. Still, he pushed on. When Hillary took the lead, the situation became perilous. Suddenly, a portion of the snowy crust broke free and slid backward about 10 feet (3 meters), carrying Hillary with it. Years of experience had taught him that the entire area was dangerous. After all, avalanches were Everest's biggest killer.

Looking backward through his legs, Hillary could see 10,000 feet (3,050 meters) down. Still, he coaxed himself forward, saying, "Ed, my boy, this is Everest—you've got to push it a bit harder!" Turning to his partner he asked, "What do you think of it, Tenzing?"

Norgay replied, "Very bad. Very dangerous."

Hillary considered a moment. "Do you think we should go on?"

Norgay answered, "Just as you wish!"

Hillary took that as a yes, and the two men struggled up the mountain until they finally reached safer snow—snow that Hillary said was like "a reprieve to a condemned man." It was at this point that they

Precious Oxygen

One thing that was absolutely critical to Hillary and Norgay's success was making sure they had enough oxygen to get up to the summit and then back down again. The night before their famous final climb, Hillary calculated that he and Norgay would each need two full bottles of oxygen, set to flow at a rate of 1 gallon (4 liters) per minute. But when Hillary checked their supply, he was alarmed to discover that two of their four bottles were only two-thirds full. At a rate of 1 gallon (4 liters) per minute, he and Norgay would have about five and a half hours of oxygen—not nearly enough to get them to the top and back down. Then Hillary considered how well he and Norgay had been climbing with the flow set at 1 gallon (4 liters) per minute. If necessary, maybe they could make their push to the summit with the oxygen set to flow at a rate of 0.8 gallon (3 liters) per minute. Hillary calculated that the lower adjustment would give them seven hours of oxygen flow—which might be just enough.

Throughout the climb, Hillary constantly had to calculate how much oxygen remained—no simple feat in the thin air at 29,000 feet (8,845 meters).

Hillary and Norgay just before making their historic final ascent to Everest's peak. Hillary once said, "I think the element of danger which is present in things like mountaineering . . . does add a tremendous amount to the challenge."

began to make really good time. Hillary cut steps into the steep icy slope, and at 9:00 a.m. they made it to the south summit—a small dome of snow and ice that stands at 28,700 feet (8,754 meters). From this vantage point, Hillary and Norgay could see almost all the way to the top.

Hillary and Norgay took a well-deserved break before tackling the next difficult section of the mountain. As they rested, Hillary checked their oxygen. Each man had used almost one entire tank. Again, Hillary

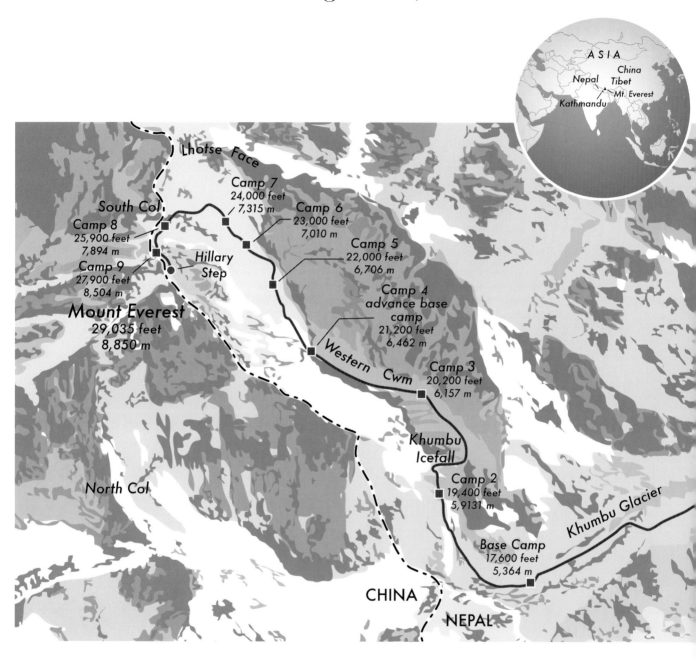

The route Hillary and Norgay took to Everest's summit.

had to calculate how much oxygen they would still need. Knowing that they would need to travel light to make it the rest of the way to the top (each tank weighed 20 pounds [9 kilograms]), Hillary decided that they should tackle the rest of the mountain carrying only one tank each.

Then Hillary and Norgay continued up the mountain. The drops on either side were enormous—up to 10,000 feet (3,050 meters). Still, Hillary was pleased to discover more safe snow. He soon became so involved in his progress that it took him a few moments to realize that Norgay was moving more slowly than usual, and his breathing was shallow and labored. A quick inspection revealed that Tenzing's oxygen tube had become clogged with ice. Luckily, Hillary was able to clear it.

In this 1996 photograph, famous Russian climber Anatoli Boukreev inches his way along the summit ridge toward the Hillary Step.

Norgay's condition improved immediately, and moments later they reached perhaps the toughest challenge of all—a 40-foot (12.2-meter) wall of ice and snow that they had seen from aerial photographs and with binoculars from Advance Base Camp.

Later Hillary wrote, "We had always thought of it as the obstacle on the ridge which could well spell defeat." But this was the point in the climb where Hillary showed that he was a mountaineer of special ability. Initial investigations showed absolutely no way up. Desperate, Hillary examined the far right side of the bluff and discovered a foot-long (0.3-meter) crack between the rock face and the nearby ice. With no other possible route, Hillary wedged himself into the cleft and wriggled and inched his way up. Today, Hillary's climb up what is now called the Hillary Step is celebrated as one of the greatest achievements in modern mountaineering. "Overcoming that rock step," Hillary has said, "made me feel the confidence that we were going to succeed." Moments later, Norgay followed and, according to Hillary, ". . . collapsed exhausted at the top like a giant fish when it has just been hauled from the sea after a terrible struggle."

But the two men did not have much time to rest. There was even more mountain to climb, looming above them. Unable to see the top, all they could do was keep going. Often, they would reach a ridge that they thought was the summit, only to discover another larger ridge stretching ahead. As Hillary put it, "Bump followed bump with maddening regularity." Exhausted, the confidence the two men had felt at the top of the Hillary Step quickly evaporated. But finally Hillary realized something: they had reached the last bump.

A few more whacks of the ice ax—a few more steps—and Edmund Hillary and Tenzing Norgay were standing on the roof of the world!

Hillary held out his hand for Norgay to shake. But the Sherpa threw his arms around Hillary and gave him a big hug. Both men admired the spectacular views. Norgay said prayers and left offerings to the gods of

Sherpa Tenzing Norgay holds an ice ax at the summit of Everest. Later, Norgay said, "At that great moment for which I had waited all my life, my mountain did not seem to me a lifeless thing of rock and ice, but warm and friendly and living."

Chomolungma. Hillary took three pictures of Tenzing, posing with flags wrapped around his ice ax. He then put the camera away, later saying, "As far as I knew, he [Norgay] had never taken a photograph before, and the summit of Everest was hardly the place to show him how."

Fifteen minutes after reaching the top of the world, Hillary and Norgay headed back down again. Though he described feeling "quiet satisfaction, and almost a little bit of surprise" at reaching the peak of Everest, Hillary felt most excited when they had "got to the bottom of the mountain again and it was all behind us." Reaching his good friend George Lowe at the peak of the South Col, Hillary announced the good news in what he called "rough New Zealand slang." He said, "We knocked the bastard off!"

SEVEN

A Life's Work

News of Hillary and Norgay's achievement reached England the same morning that Queen Elizabeth II was to be crowned. Hunched over a tiny radio at Base Camp, Hillary and the rest of the crew heard the British Broadcasting Company (BBC) interrupt the queen's coronation to announce, "We have great pleasure in announcing that the British Everest expedition has finally reached the summit of Mt. Everest."

At that moment Hillary felt the full impact of what he had accomplished. "If the BBC announces it," he said, "it must be right."

On the slow trek from Base Camp back to Kathmandu, Hillary and Norgay slowly came to understand the enormity of their accomplishment. Well-wishers cheered. Mail carriers brought congratulatory letters. One day John Hunt handed Hillary a letter that was addressed to Sir Edmund Hillary K.B.E.—Knight Commander of the British Empire. Queen Elizabeth had dubbed him a knight. Embarrassed, Hillary told

Sir John Hunt and Sir Edmund Hillary at a reception after being greeted by the queen of England.

one reporter that he did not feel like "knightly material," saying:

> I regarded it all as a bit of a joke . . . I realized that we had done quite
> well, but we just climbed a mountain. It didn't warrant all the reac-
> tion that there had been from the world. I've tried to maintain that
> attitude ever since. These challenges are great, and they are very sat-
> isfying, but they are certainly not the beginning or end of the world.

Despite his resistance to his newfound fame, Edmund Hillary's image was soon reproduced on stamps, books, magazine covers, and the New Zealand five-dollar bill. Naturally modest, both Hillary and Norgay—who quickly became a hero throughout India, Tibet, and Nepal—were embarrassed by their notoriety and continued to credit the entire team for the expedition's success. But despite their best efforts to share the glory, the world community continued to heap its praise on the two men who had reached the top.

The celebration followed Hillary and Norgay all the way to Kathmandu. The entire team was met by the king and queen of Nepal and Prime Minister Jawaharlal Nehru of India. In England, Hillary and John

A Team Effort

As Hillary and Norgay greeted supporters on their way back to Kathmandu, a controversy arose. Members of the Indian and Nepali media began to suggest that Norgay had been the one to reach the summit first. As reporters harassed them with questions, both climbers grew more and more uncomfortable. According to Hillary, "the question of who reaches the top of a mountain first is completely unimportant to the climbers involved." Accordingly, both Hillary and Norgay stressed that their success was a team effort. But when the press continued to push for an answer, even though Hillary had been a few steps ahead, Hillary and Norgay said that they had reached the summit at the exact same time.

A group photo of the 1953 Mount Everest expedition. (Hillary is in the back row, fifth from the left; Norgay is seventh from the left.)

Hunt were officially knighted. Hillary was in a perfect position to cash in on his name and accomplishment and live a relatively easy life. But that was not Hillary's style.

Even when I was standing on the summit of Everest I looked across the valley to another one of the great peaks, called Makalu . . . and as I stood there, I mentally picked out a route on this great unclimbed mountain. Everest for me was more a beginning than an end.

One new adventure was marriage. Soon after his return to New Zealand, Hillary married Louise Rose, an old friend. In 1954 Peter Hillary, now a well-respected climber in his own right, was born. A family man, Edmund Hillary settled back into the beekeeping business with his brother.

But it was not long before other adventures lured him away again. Hillary was soon invited to join a trip across Antarctica led by the British explorer Sir Vivian Fuchs. Fuchs's goal was to travel across the entire continent by tractor—something that had never been done. The plan was simple: Fuchs would leave from Shackleton Base near the Weddell Sea and travel to the South Pole. At the same time, Hillary and a New Zealand team would start on the opposite side of the continent at Scott Base on McMurdo Sound and also make their way to the pole. Then Fuchs and his team would continue across the continent using the route that Hillary had established.

Though hesitant at first, Hillary finally decided to join and left for Antarctica in 1955, just months after the birth of his second child, a daughter named Sarah. After establishing a winter base on the edge of Antarctica, Hillary and his team headed across the icy continent over terrain similar to the Khumbu Icefall. As Hillary remembered, "We dropped tractors down a number of crevasses but always managed to pull them out again without anybody coming to harm." On

Hillary and family in 1962. From left are his son Peter, Hillary, daughter Belinda, wife Louise, and daughter Sarah. "We took our family into the out-of-doors," Hillary said. "We swam and we clambered around the hills."

December 15, 1957, Hillary established a final camp 500 miles (805 kilometers) from the South Pole. At this point, Hillary learned that Fuchs's team was expecting to reach the pole sometime between Christmas and New Year's Day. The original plan called for Hillary to leave supplies for Fuchs's team and then turn back. Ahead of schedule and slightly bored, Hillary's adventurous spirit got the best of him, and he decided to continue all the way to the South Pole. He said later, "I've never been all that good at sticking to plans." Hillary reached the South Pole on January 4, 1958, before Fuchs's team. Hillary then did what he could to help Fuchs's team complete a successful journey to the pole and then across the entire continent themselves.

In 1960, Hillary set off on another adventure, returning to the Himalayas to search for signs of the *yeti*—more commonly known as the Abominable Snowman. At the time, there was some evidence that a species of gorilla or bear lived in hiding higher up than any humans did. But after examining everything from alleged *yeti* tracks to assorted animal scalps, Hillary concluded that the *yeti* was mythical. Still, Hillary viewed the expedition as a decided success. It was this trip back to the Himalayas that set him on the path of his true life work: helping the Sherpa people.

In the late 1950s and early 1960s the Sherpas lived a very simple rustic life. They had no medical facilities, no indoor plumbing, and no schools. In 1961, Hillary asked the head Sherpa on his expedition, "If there's something we can do for the Sherpas, what should it be?"

The reply was immediate: "What we would like is for our children in Khunde village to have a school."

That was all Hillary needed to hear. Within months he had set up the Himalayan Trust, an organization whose charter was to raise money for projects to improve life in Sherpa villages. Through the years, the trust has funded thirty schools, two hospitals, twelve medical clinics, and numerous bridges and airfields. In recent years, funds have been raised to rebuild monasteries and to replant trees in the valleys and along the slopes of the Mustang, Khumbu, and Pokhara regions. Understandably, "Ed" as he's known to the Sherpa people, takes great pride in his good works.

> *I don't know if I particularly want to be remembered for anything. I have enjoyed great satisfaction from my climb of Everest and my trips to the poles. But there's no doubt, either, that my most worthwhile things have been the building of schools and medical clinics. That has given me more satisfaction than a footprint on a mountain.*

Family was another of the great satisfactions in Hillary's life. He and Louise eventually had a third child, Belinda, born in 1960. Living in New Zealand, the family took many camping trips and lived for a time in the Himalayas. Hillary called it "A very full and very happy existence."

Then, in 1975, tragedy struck. While flying from Kathmandu to a dedication ceremony for a new school, Louise and Belinda were killed in a small plane crash. For Hillary it was "an absolute disaster." Anguished, he soon discovered that the only way he could attempt to get over the horrible loss was to "carry on very energetically, doing the things that we had all been doing together." In the years following Louise and Belinda's deaths, Hillary continued his efforts on behalf of the Sherpa people. He also embarked on a new expedition. In 1977, he and a small group that included his son, Peter, journeyed by speedboat over the entire length of the Ganges River.

Still other adventures followed. In 1985 Hillary accompanied Neil Armstrong, the first man to stand on the moon, on a small twin-engined plane to the North Pole. This feat made Hillary the only known person to have stood on both poles and reached the summit of Everest. Also in 1985, Hillary was appointed the New Zealand High Commissioner to India, Nepal, and Bangladesh and spent four and a half years in New Delhi. During this time, he continued his good works and construction projects in Nepal. In 1990, Hillary married a lifetime friend named June Mulgrew.

As he has grown older, Hillary has become a passionate advocate for Everest itself. Today, many people want to climb the great mountain. For prices up to $70,000, a relatively inexperienced climber can join an expedition and maybe even reach the top. Since the period of time every year that Everest can be climbed is limited to a few weeks in the late spring, the mountain has become extremely crowded. Though most expeditions now cart out their trash, Hillary feels strongly that the mountain is overused and that the Nepalese government should restrict

Hillary and his second wife, June, in Kathmandu to celebrate the fiftieth anniversary of Hillary and Norgay's famous climb. "When we were climbing in those early days," Hillary has said, "we were the only people there. . . . I feel lucky to have been up there climbing when it was a different sort of mountaineering."

the number of climbing groups given access each year. He has even rec-ommended that the Nepalese government shut Everest down for five years to let the mountain's plant life regenerate. Hillary has used some of the funds from the Himalayan Trust to plant tree nurseries and to start projects aimed at preventing soil erosion.

Afterword

Through the years, Edmund Hillary has grown more and more thankful that he had a chance to climb the great mountains of the world when they were completely untamed. As he puts it, "now they have thousands of feet of fixed ropes in all the difficult places. They have 60 aluminum ladders on the ice fall." More and more climbers use those ladders every year. In the spring of 2003, the season leading up to the fiftieth anniversary of Hillary and Norgay's famous climb, a record sixty-five expeditions were expected on the mountain. A climber named Lhakpa Gela set a speed record, reaching the summit from Base Camp in 10 hours 56 minutes 46 seconds. Ming Kipa, a fifteen-year-old Sherpa girl, became the youngest person to reach the top. And two days before the anniversary, Sibusiso Vilane of Swaziland became the first black person to make it to the summit.

To mark the fiftieth anniversary of the climb, Hillary turned down an invitation from the queen of England so that he could be in the Himalayas with the Sherpa people he loves. As he has said, "I came to the Himalayas for the mountains, and stayed for the people." Hillary and June rode through the Kathmandu streets in a horse-drawn carriage, past cheering crowds. Children held up signs that read, "May God give us strength to be like you." Though he walks with the aid of a hiking stick, Hillary gave speeches and greeted old friends with great enthusiasm.

As he faces the end of his life, Edmund Hillary retains his characteristic modesty. In 1998, he summed up his career at the annual American Himalayan Foundation dinner:

> *I was just an average bloke. . . . And try as I did, there was no way to destroy my heroic image. But as I learned through the years, as long as you didn't believe all that rubbish about yourself, you wouldn't come to much harm.*

As seen towering above Base Camp, Mount Everest still remains the ultimate challenge to a new generation of climbers.

EDMUND HILLARY
AND HIS TIMES

1919   Edmund Hillary is born in Tuakau, New Zealand.

1936   He takes a class trip to Mount Ruapehu, south of Auckland, and first discovers his love of the outdoors.

1939   He goes to a tourist resort, The Hermitage, and climbs Mount Olivier.

1942   He becomes a navigator in the New Zealand Air Force.

1946   He befriends Harry Ayres, New Zealand's best-known mountaineer.

1951   He makes his first trip to the Himalayas with George Lowe and a team of New Zealand climbers.

He joins famous climber Eric Shipton to explore a new southern approach to Mount Everest.

1952   A team of Swiss climbers reaches 28,000 feet (8,540 meters) up Everest but is forced back.

1953   Edmund Hillary and Tenzing Norgay become the first men to climb to the summit of Mount Everest.

He marries Louise Rose in Auckland, New Zealand.

1957   He joins a team of explorers led by Sir Vivian Fuchs whose goal is to travel across Antarctica by tractor.

1960   He returns to the Himalayas to search for signs of the *yeti* or the Abominable Snowman.

1961   He establishes the Himalayan Trust, an organization dedicated to raising money for projects to improve life in Sherpa villages.

1975   Edmund Hillary's wife and daughter Belinda are killed in a small plane crash.

1977   Edmund Hillary and his son, Peter, lead a small group down the Ganges River by jet boat.

1986   Tenzing Norgay dies.

1990   Edmund Hillary marries a lifetime friend, June Mulgrew.

2003   He turns down an invitation from the queen of England, so he can celebrate the fiftieth anniversary of his historic climb with the Sherpa people.

Further Research

Books

Brennan, Christine. *Sir Edmund Hillary: Modern-Day Explorer.* Broomall, PA: Chelsea House, 2000.

Coburn, Broughton. *Triumph on Everest: A Photobiography of Sir Edmund Hillary.* Washington, D.C.: National Geographic, 2000.

Hillary, Edmund. *View from the Summit.* United States: Pocket, 2000.

Ramsay, Cynthia Russ. *Sir Edmund Hillary and the People of Everest.* Kansas City, MO: Andrews McMeel, 2002.

Stewart, Whitney. *Sir Edmund Hillary: To Everest and Beyond.* Minneapolis: Lerner, 1996.

Web Sites

Everest 50

www.nationalgeographic.com/everest/

First to Summit

www.pbs.org/wgbh/nova/everest/history/firstsummit.html

A Man to Match His Mountain

www.salon.com/bc/1998/12/cov_01bc.html

Edmund Hillary and Tenzing Norgay

www.time.com/time/time100/heroes/profile/hillary_norgay01.html

Bibliography

Bonnington, Chris. *Everest, The Hard Way.* New York: Random House, 1976.

Bonnington, Chris, and Audrey Salkeld, eds. *Heroic Climbs.* Seattle: The Mountaineers, 1994.

Boukreev, Anatoli, and G. Weston DeWalt. *The Climb.* New York: St. Martin's, 1997.

Hillary, Edmund. *From the Ocean to the Sky.* New York: Viking, 1979.

———. *High Adventure.* New York: E. P. Dutton, 1955.

———. *Nothing Venture, Nothing Win.* New York: Coward, McCann & Geoghegan, 1975.

Jenkins, Steve. *The Top of the World, Climbing Mount Everest.* Boston: Houghton Mifflin, 1999.

Krakauer, Jon. *Into Thin Air.* New York: Random House, 1997.

Ortner, Sherry B. *Life and Death on Mt. Everest.* Princeton, NJ: Princeton University Press, 2001.

Stewart, Whitney. *Sir Edmund Hillary: To Everest and Beyond.* Minneapolis: Lerner, 1996.

Source Notes

Foreword:

p. 6: "I was just an enthusiastic mountaineer of modest abilities who. . . ." Edmund Hillary, speaking at American Himalayan Foundation Annual Dinner, November 5, 1998.

p. 6: "Here is a someone who did the near impossible, climbing the world's tallest mountain. . . ." Don George, writing in *Salon* magazine.

Chapter 1:

pp. 7–8: "There was a phase when I was the fastest gun in the west, then another when I explored the Antarctic. I would walk. . . ." Edmund Hillary, interview, San Francisco, November 16, 1991.

p. 9: "What will they send me next!" Whitney Stewart, *Sir Edmund Hillary: To Everest and Beyond* (Minneapolis: Lerner, 1996), p. 21.

p. 9: "I was a shy boy with a deep sense of inferiority that I still have." Hillary, interview, 1991.

p. 9: "I always felt my father wanted me to admit that. . . ." Interview with Hillary, *Outside* magazine, October 1999.

p. 9: "Much of Edmund's determination came from standing up to his father." Stewart, p. 18.

p. 9: "people of very strong character." Hillary, interview, 1991.

p. 9: "Remember the starving millions in Asia." Hillary, interview, 1991.

p. 10: "I had no friends whatsoever." Hillary, interview, 1991.

p. 14: "This was the first time I had even seen snow, because we didn't get it in Auckland, and for ten days. . . ." Hillary, interview, 1991.

p. 14: "Whenever he was in a difficult circumstance which he frequently was. . . ." Hillary, interview, 1991.

p. 14: "There are some people who are natural leaders, who have the ability to think quickly. . . ." Hillary, interview, 1991.

Source Notes

Chapter 2:

p. 16: "It took two years of university life to convince my parents that I was unsuited to an academic career." Edmund Hillary, *High Adventure* (New York: E. P. Dutton, 1955), p. 14.

p. 16: "a constant fight against the vagaries of the weather and a mad rush. . . . " *High Adventure*, p. 14.

p. 18: "I was pretty tired when we got to the icecap, but Harry was like a tiger and almost dragged me to the top." *High Adventure*, p. 15.

p. 20: "And next day I returned home, but my new enthusiasm. . . . " *High Adventure*, p. 16.

p. 20: "Have you ever thought about going to the Himalayas, Ed?": *High Adventure*, p. 17.

p. 22: "We returned to Ranikhet thin and wasted and without a penny in our pockets. . . . " *High Adventure*, p. 20.

Chapter 3:

p. 26: "If he had succeeded in getting to the top I think it would be fantastic. . . . " Hillary, interview, *Outside* magazine.

p. 28: "Sitting in his sleeping bag, with his umbrella over his head to divert the drips. . . . " *High Adventure*, p. 38.

p. 28: "the horror photograph." *High Adventure*, p. 40.

p. 30: "Because the climbing route wove under, around, and between hundreds of these unstable towers. . . . " Jon Krakauer, *Into Thin Air*. (New York: Random House, 1997), p. 76.

Chapter 4:

p. 33: "Evidence of Hunt's caliber was not long in appearing. . . . " *High Adventure*, p. 125.

p. 34: "lead the expedition from the front." *High Adventure*, p. 126.

p. 35: "quiet air of confidence." *High Adventure*, p. 126.

p. 35: "The Swiss parties had been strong ones, well equipped and well organized. . . ." *High Adventure*, p. 123–124.

p. 38: "You're so much slower in higher altitudes . . . but I used to keep moving pretty steadily most of the time. . . ." Hillary, interview, 1991.

p. 39: "innumerable crevasses and menaced by crumbling ice towers. . . ." *High Adventure*, p. 131.

p. 40: "rope work was first class, as my near-catastrophe had shown. . . . Best of all, as far as I was concerned, he was prepared to go fast and hard." *High Adventure*, p. 154.

Chapter 5:

p. 41: "Without a doubt our greatest strength on Everest in 1953 was our very strong team. . . ." Hillary, interview, *Outside* magazine.

p. 43: "I could, if necessary, have gone on a great deal farther." *High Adventure*, p. 162.

p. 45: "Towering above our heads was our mountain, looking depressingly steep and formidable." *High Adventure*, p. 179.

p. 46: "They're up! They're up!" *High Adventure*, p. 181.

p. 46: "sensible chaps with a keen desire to go on living. . . ." *High Adventure*, p. 181.

pp. 48–49: "each step became a separate entity—a major task that was going to require a maximum of effort." *High Adventure*, p. 205.

p. 49: "This demonstration of loyalty and unselfishness from a man who was obviously going to have great difficulty. . . ." *High Adventure*, p. 207.

Chapter 6:

p. 52: "the flesh is weak and I decided on a comfortable night." *High Adventure*, p. 214.

p. 53: "Ed, my boy, this is Everest—you've got to push it a bit harder!" *High Adventure*, p. 223.

p. 53: "a reprieve to a condemned man." *High Adventure*, p. 223.

p. 58: "We had always thought of it as the obstacle on the ridge which could well spell defeat." *High Adventure*, p. 227.

p. 59: "Overcoming that rock step, made me feel the confidence that we were going to succeed." Hillary, interview, 1991.

p. 59: ". . . collapsed exhausted at the top like a giant fish when it has just been hauled from the sea after a terrible struggle." *Into Thin Air*, p. 17.

p. 59: "Bump followed bump with maddening regularity." *High Adventure*, p. 231.

p. 59: "As far as I knew, he had never taken a photograph before, and. . . ." *High Adventure*, p. 233.

p. 59: "quiet satisfaction, and almost a little bit of surprise" Hillary, interview, 1991.

p. 59: "got to the bottom of the mountain again and it was all behind us." Katherine Mansfield, *Adventurers: Sir Edmund Hillary, King of the World*, http://www.nzedge.com/heroes/hillary.html

p. 59: "rough New Zealand slang." *High Adventure*, p. 241.

Chapter 7:

p. 60: "We have great pleasure in announcing that the British Everest expedition has finally reached the summit of Mt. Everest." Hillary, interview, 1991.

p. 60: "If the BBC announces it, it must be right." Hillary, interview, 1991.

p. 61: "I regarded it all as a bit of a joke . . . I realized that we had done quite well, but we just climbed. . . ." Hillary, interview, *Outside* magazine.

p. 62: "the question of who reaches the top of a mountain first is completely unimportant. . . ." Hillary, interview, *Outside* magazine.

p. 63: "Even when I was standing on the summit of Everest I looked across the valley. . . ." Hillary, interview, *Outside* magazine.

p. 63: "We dropped tractors down a number of crevasses but always managed. . . ." Hillary, interview, *Outside* magazine.

p. 64: "I've never been all that good at sticking to plans." Hillary, Interview, 1991.

p. 64: "If there's something we can do for the Sherpas, what should it be?" Hillary, interview, *Outside* magazine.

p. 64: "What we would like is for our children in Khunde village to have a school." Hillary, interview, *Outside* magazine.

p. 65: "I don't know if I particularly want to be remembered for anything. I have enjoyed great satisfaction. . . ." *Adventurers.*

p. 66: "A very full and very happy existence." Hillary, interview, 1991.

p. 66: "an absolute disaster." Hillary, interview, 1991.

p. 66: "carry on very energetically, doing the things that we had all been doing together." Hillary, interview, 1991.

Afterword:

p. 68: "now they have thousands of feet of fixed ropes in all the difficult places. . . ." The Mountain Zone Web site, *Sir Edmund Hillary and the Legends of Modern Climbing History*, November 8, 1996.

p. 69: "May God give us strength to be like you." *The New York Times*, May 28, 2003, p. A9.

p. 69: "I was just an average bloke. . . . And try as I did, there was no way to destroy my heroic image. But as I learned. . . ." Edmund Hillary, American Himalayan Foundation Annual Dinner, November 5, 1998.

INDEX

Page numbers in **boldface** are illustrations.